To Deborah - Wish you color, movement, music and joy. You remain a foundation of my life here, and your friendship continues to be a blessing

Teaching a Man to Unstick His Tail

beyond measure. With love + admiration;

Ralph Hamilton

Sibling Rivalry Press
Little Rock, Arkansas
www.siblingrivalrypress.com

Teaching a Man to Unstick His Tail
Copyright © 2015 by Ralph Hamilton

Cover art: Detail from *Sunday Morning-Eight Legs* by Lucian Freud.
Used with permission of the Art Institute of Chicago.
Author photo by Chris Walker
Cover design by Bob Faust, Faust Associates

Sibling Rivalry Press, LLC
PO Box 26147
Little Rock, AR 72221
info@siblingrivalrypress.com

www.siblingrivalrypress.com

ISBN: 978-1-937420-88-8

Library of Congress Control Number: 2014959475

First Sibling Rivalry Press Edition, March 2015

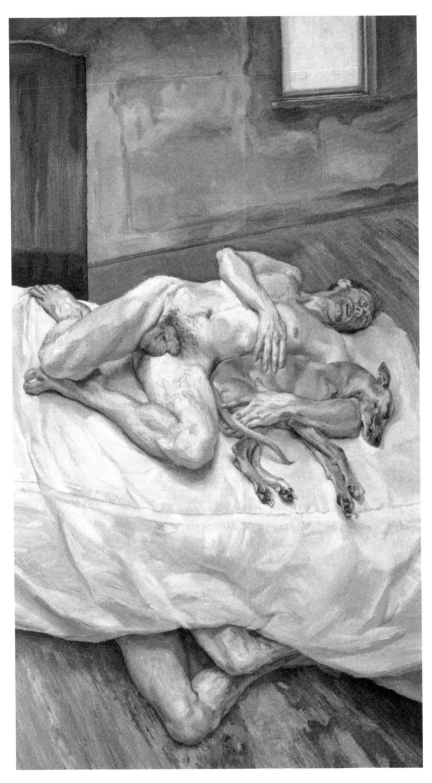

Sunday Morning-Eight Legs by Lucian Freud

To Coleman Brown

So Grateful

As our blood labors to beget
    Spirits, as like souls as it can,
Because such fingers need to knit
    That subtle knot which makes us man

from *The Ecstasy* by John Donne

Us, Explained

Leaving our car behind to enter the woods—
before nine days of trails, of tachycardial climbs,

before a rain-drowned night on the mountain's
north face, our tent bound unwisely to what passed

for a tree (and yes, there was lightning), before
blisters, torn shoulders, the fear we were lost,

before mule shit, squirrel shit, elk shit and deer, the shits
of cougar, coyote (or was it wolf?), before you screamed

you couldn't get clean in the cold turquoise stream. Yes,
though fine ursid fruits were everywhere heaped—lustrous,

whiskered, ropey and blackberry blue—before we failed
to find even one bear. And after.

PENTIMENTO

Most chairs and the Chinese lamps sit
undisturbed, along with three kilims
you left. Yet the kitchen table you stripped

and stained the year we met, you took
with the abstract impasto that hung

in the hall, motley blues and whites
with black threads bearding its spackled
words like hairs on a suspect mole. Gone

also the large sepia oil you modeled after
Leonardo's lower-trunk study of light

on cloth. And the first gift I gave
you, a skewed indigo sky scumbled
on board (we never framed), that

too. Now certain walls gawp
oddly blank as if we'd never noticed

something was missing or had somehow
run out of nails. How long had they
been part of these walls? Twelve years?

Ten? So constant the pictures
got lost in paint. Possession is

nothing. But absence has breath,
has bones, a hue, your scent in
silence still moist on the stairs.

LOVESONG

cento from Sappho

dewfall   dawn with small golden feet
straight slender trees   come to your grove
I lie alone   come out of Crete
and find me here   come to me as you came
long ago   come down   come now

the rose-and-violet crowns I wove
into your hair   come down to black earth
horses stand amid flowers and graze
the wind glad and sweet   come now
I turn greener than grass   come here

I loved you once   gave you a white
goat   your face all laughter   nothing
takes its place   percussion salt and honey
a quivering   spread wide   come out
after so long   I dream   come soon

wash off all that wrong   salt-bitter sea
tangled parsley   things made of worry
let us have no pain   no mourning   I lie
alone   speak out   I am willing   weaker
than water   should you be willing   come

my tongue sticks to my dry mouth   living
nor dead   I am calling out   loose me
from black dreams   old woman's flesh   this
narrow between   dusk sifts down   I
don't know where   trembling

Grown Up

I'd like to think it didn't mean much
although he hadn't yet moved out
when I peed in my ex-partner's toilet

at 3 a.m. while he was away, or that
I was merely marking my turf
dog-style, albeit I didn't stand to aim

the stream. I'd prefer to admit I'm
middle-aged with a peanut-sized bladder
and simply chose the closest pot

but his is farther. Fact is, I sat in
the dark just to breathe his air, to be
where he'd been like a movie-dog

lying down at Boot Hill on his master's
grave. Even as a kid I worried
what happened when a film crew left:

Did the dog stay long? Who fed
him? Was the mutt consoled by his
cowboy's boots? I should've stolen

one of my ex's shoes, slunk back to
my room to tear it apart with my
teeth, except I couldn't afford new

veneers without his insurance. Playing
with my brother when we were boys,
one of us would bark *En garde!* as

we dueled while peeing above an open
commode. We slashed our swords
with swashbuckling panache—blades

splashed, sparked gold before being
spent—oblivious then that a grown-up,
finally, must mop up the mess.

Negative Space

With homemade shiv
                   the shaving of soap

Pare excess to find form
                   dormant within—now chisel, now
          rounding
                        now runnel, now
                                        notch

Let blade query bar like wind
                        worries rock, quarry what
          comes next

Might this knife somehow sense   how much
                        to excise?

                   Could my hand carve
          a totem
                             it shudders to touch?

          Or is the reveal, like me
     without you:
                   whatever   remains—

THE MOTHER, BROKEN

semi-cento from Charles Olson & John Berryman

1.

I have had to learn the simplest things last
First you break
Main Street is deserted
The heart is a clock
Grief is fatiguing

2.

I am a vain man
I've never been good at math
            or gluing bits back together
I don't know one damn butterfly from another
It shouldn't be hard to believe damage is final
I have strained everything except my ears

3.

When mother broke I tried but not too hard
The heart is a cloak
I hunt among stones
The only way I'll ever be whole, milky
            & smooth like seaglass
I am two eyes   a pelican of lies
Cling to me & I promise you'll drown
Love me love me love me

4.

Is being broken into more & more parts, fine
            & sharp as sifted sand, democratic
            as dust, really the end

How small is this news
I'm only a glass, says the glass: Sometimes
       I hold the sea, sometimes the sun, though
       never more than this dark wine—
Break me

SLIDE

It begins with a skinny-dipping college kid
who slipped and slid one pool down to the next,
to the next, slick and shouting to the next
above Glen Falls, gathering two then three then
four until sweeping five of his friends
over, all but one to their deaths. The living and
dead were brought to the emergency room
where I worked that summer at just their age—
I remember wailing and the EMTs' jokes—
when I learned the first time how one loss
tumbles into the next.

Today on the radio I hear an interview
with a poet whose child was murdered.
The poem she reads in a measured voice
rehearses her daughter's death, her hope
the killer's eyes were not the girl's last sight.
But I've stopped breathing—sliding—
wondering what my brother saw as he laid on
the bare park table, if quail flushed, a hawk
skirled, if clouds clung low or scudded distant
till disappeared, about the taste of metal and
oil, what thoughts filled his fingers as they

gripped the gun, the barrel's brief weight
at rest on his tongue. I will buy this poet's
book. Won't open it. It will lie on a table
I circle for weeks, picking it up once or
again, cautiously, as if slippery or poison, as if
prodding a snake. I will almost think, *It isn't real
until I read it*, as if I could stall or even change
the poems, their plot. Eventually I may
skim one poem, another, later two more,
then likely five. And I'll hear boys laughing
above a fall.

STEPHEN HAWKING IN LOVE

First, accept the impossible—
light is particle, light is wave,
(or maybe not) hence capable
of behaving like both

*

In love, distance, the question
of necessary breath between: If not
static union, the cosmological
constant wavers from & to

*

If flesh is a *field* & desire a *force*,
Unified Theory holds that bodies
mediate love, though fiction prefers
hearts as the medium of fusion

*

Third, accept the impossible—there
is lack, there is full: Each moves
through marriage concurrent &/or
in sequence, never only, never done

*

Stars, yes, but no matter dies, energy
& love merely entangle, transmute,
not dispersed nor finally dissolved,
existing in no one form forever

*

The crook of desire, its seesaw
swing, made not for balance
just joy of motion: Rise always
preceding a necessary thud

*

In the deep laws of space, other
realities are harder to avoid than
find—thus somewhere the one
I love is loving me back

PALS

There is a Gumby
in us all who knows
with all his bendy
boneless brain that
play with Pokey
and Pokey's play
with him oblige
them, willy-nilly,
to bow and torque
and tilt. It's why
arms and tail are
PVC, why their spines
need never snap
when playing too
hard, when playing
too mean, why even
fifty-four years on
in the privacy of
an attic box, Gumby
still pokes Pokey
and when no one's
near, Pokey still
pokes him. It's oh
so sick. Still I crane
to hear: *Give-it-up-*
you-wedge-head-
freak! So familiar,
the perfect pretzel
logic that keeps even
plastic palsy-walsy
and pliant. By four
years old I loved
Play Doh's sweet smell

too, its crayon hues,
soft-silk stretch and all
the things I shaped—
sausagey trees, whole
houses, roly-poly
families and pets. Even
so, left out too long
things formed grow
hard, and overnight
they crack.

SONNET I
Berrigan cento

The air beginning to thicken
each sleeping son is broke-backed and dumb
no such thing as a breakdown   not this day
they believe this   not me
so he digs   it hurts   and the dog
days come   littered with soups
cigarette butts   the heavy innocence
of childhood   marvelous dirty days   dressed
in newspaper   wan as pale thighs
aching to be fucked   it hurts   so he digs
to the big promise of emptiness   coffee   my arms
goodbye!   goodbye!   goodbye!
it was summer   ripeness corrupting every tree
everything turning   in this light to stones

Snowblind

Conceive
of your skis'
trail through

new snow as
two lines drawn
in graphite

across thick white
paper. The
lane each

blade carves
extends so
far and close

without inter-
secting that
it's hard to

discern where
either could
part, if their

ends ever
veer for one,
four, even

twenty years.
Viewed from
a distance

these parallel
paths seem
to converge.

Later if you're
game, erase
the first

track (or
second if you
wish). The rut

that remains
marks the same
route, still

charts the
same course.
But in stereo

sight on a
field like white
paper

the one left
behind
appears to

drift

METANOIA

for Liam

We need to touch
each other
to make him dead.
It's animal
really, this need to
bring muzzle
to muzzle, breathe
each other's
anxious scent, to lick
a block of salt
together—

BIRD LIFE

You are a chicken and
I am a chicken. Neither
of us knew which one came
first, but together we
made a comely farmyard
couple. Oh how we cackled
and ooh did we cluck—
you roistered me, I
roostered you—till we laid

a perfect pullet to-
gether. I sat on the nest
and I sat on the nest: I
coddled that egg much
more than required. Yet
the egg failed to
thrive and the egg
failed to hatch. When
finally cracked open

it stank. Though biddies
may squat, big chickens don't
cry: We quail, we lark, we
snipe, we brood. Hence queer
old hens—forgive me, same-
gendered fowl—require more
than cocks and much more
than good lays to make life
gay together.

PRAYER FOR SPRING
semi-cento from John Ashbery

White sunlight
on the polished floor
and windows closed:
How night ends.
But you will not listen.
—Day again.
Leaden. Soon another
lid of clouds and
shuddering pages,
an icy lake blown back
to fore (winter's mode
of obfuscation) facts
unbound beneath
plain sight, more
and more less
deep, as if a door
opened, offered only
after. Where we are.—
Put away the book.
First, coffee. Breathe.
How light parts: A fork.
A spoon. Separate
lives. I've not been
here, this salt white
room where words
blow through—one life,
another, majesty
and mush, a year
made mash,
the street's muffled
hum, and snow
like crushed paper
scattered and heaped
against the glass.

WHAT I MISSED

Like eager Xmas mornings—the tinsel
and torn paper, gingerbread men with green

jujube buttons I loved to suck, the smell
of sap, Perry Como's *Jingle Bells* and red socks

worn just once a year—that suddenly end.
Though the holiday, at least, returns

even if what comes turns out to be a stranger
thing, always less than I imagined. Why mourn

a man I never loved, if neither did I wholly
not? Some other thing, not really friendship

either—the careful queries and tacit assents,
our taboo topics, much closer sometimes

to marriage—till my fingers traced the thick vein
of his neck and all we made ourselves forget.

I remember a large package one boyhood
Xmas, sashed in red ribbon and candy cane

paper amid frenzied unbinding. It looked
like everything I'd ever wanted. Without pause

I opened the box, only to find it wasn't
meant for me. *It's like that,* I say to myself

as I stare at the phone, *Never mine.*

How the Skink Regrows its Tail

Years happen   elsewhere
                              their selvage
              frays
                   & holes
                                                grow wide:

              Too acid too hot
                        we fall apart   forget how to fold

       too cool too lean   we self-consume
                                   maybe worse   do not

                                        *

What is the knot   where loss
                         of adhesion of curl

                                       where more warp
                              more wear

              overtakes   repair—

                   the constant of
                                        cells &
                                   long marriage

                                        *

Moth dust   oils   danders
                   of desire

37

trapped
in grooves of sticky fingers
yellow as nicotine

a residue of
seconds   defaults
of obligatory lies

*

While proteins go bad   & cells decay
daily

the clumping of hurt
like lint
in a dryer   the shower drain

clotted
with resentments of hair

*

Mass remains
steady
despite   distension

a transit   to silence

distance within
grown large
& rumors

of loneliness
feed   on themselves

*

Till lysosomes come   comb the remains

               salvage
                    scrap   & braid

       new cells—a constant
                  devotion: I

                         die each

         hour & every three days   grow
                  a new heart

Spooning

The Right is right, when queens become kings
the country's gone to hell. Let's sue Serta
for ruining our marriage. Location,
location: Didn't we learn? Lebensraum, Manifest
Destiny, four-car McMansions, forty acres
and a mule. Not mine, but ours. Not bigger,
better! *I can't sleep*, you said before you bought
the new bed. Now we're boxers in opposite
corners, Blues and Grays, Reds and Blues,
demanding our own downy Singapore, Sultanate,
Liechtenstein or 'Stan. Weren't we happier in
a full-sized world? As beds grow bigger, our union
shrinks, both so damned fat we text each other
across wastelands of thousand-count Egyptian thread.
Even twins weren't so bad—the Club of Rome
screamed limits, never anomie. Let's down-size,
regress, make Schumacher our muse. No Castros
to convert here (how many backs were broken
for that revolution?). Just elbows, sharp toenails,
stale breath, two dogs, leg twitch, cold feet,
one cat and an apnea mask.

Our Summer
Lowell cento

we   and you
back and forth

without a center

the sky descending
all shops closed

dark swallows

back and forth
doubtless come back

without a center

and I   still
between

With(out) Him

In the yard outside my window is a blue rhinoceros, a blue
rhinoceros afloat in my yard. Perhaps he's part whale, perhaps
barracuda, the blue rhinoceros with small-set eyes, set so far
apart. I watch him all day, though he seems unaware. He lolls
in the shallows on green velvet moss, on rockweed, sargassum,
on plankton and dulse, a great hair-horned brute in blue-gray
shadows that ripple, that wave like large sea fans, like large sea
fans in my backyard. He preys on my mind. Will he breach,
will he spout, does he graze among coral, strain krill from
the grass, the blue rhinoceros on my velvet lawn? I would
stroke him and feed him if he would allow, might fondle his
snout, I'd tickle wee ears that rise from his hump. It may be
I love him. No doubt that's absurd. Besides, I'm afraid of the
tar-eyed beast now backstroking my yard. Because if startled
he could capsize my house, could deflate my lungs with his
horn, with hoof weight, with the butt of his head. Or else
dive down deep, like a whale he might sound to dire sable
depths below bluestone and sod in my broad backyard. From
there he might vanish, may very well vanish and never return
from waves, from moss, from the vast callous reef engulfing
my lot. Without him I'm lost. Like water, he's boundless. I
drink him like air.

MOTHER'S STROKE

burnt umber eyes
                     bluing now
     become her tongue

WEIGHT

This humid afternoon

all earth's humors
exhume themselves in

tight tin soldier

drill. The air is
oil, humus,

glue, the trees gangrene,

my breathing thick as
rheum: A man might

pray for plain dry dirt,

dry wind, dry cold to
void his weight,

break particle, pith,

his front and frets,
to humdrum spoor,

ordinary human dust.

CLEAN WOOD BOX
cento from Sylvia Plath & Ted Hughes

Love set going like a fat gold watch—we enter as animals.
Your story. My story. Little poppies, little hell flames.
A wisp of your hair, your pink wool dress. Perfection is terrible.

Between locusts and honey, all your poems still to be found.
We only did what poetry told us to do that Monday.
Viciousness in the kitchen. We enter as animals.

Potatoes hiss derision, mud—happy to be martyred.
Two, of course there are two: Little poppies, little hell flames.
The Sunday lamb cracks in its fat. Perfection—terrible.

Poems, like smoking entrails, came soft into your hands.
Our Eden caught and devoured you that Monday.
Help me, you whispered. *We enter as animals.*

The yew's black fingers, slender and dead.
Your story. My story. Little poppies, little hell flames.
The hare in the bowl screamed, *Perfection is terrible.*

The hill steps off into whiteness. And all your poems still.
Sucked the oxygen out of us both. Little poppies. Little hell flames.
Love set going like a fat gold watch: Enter as animals.
A wisp of hair, your pink dress. Perfection. Terrible.

Sisters

Another kind of love
is what you called it.
We'll be sisters, sort of,
gain vaginas without losing

our cocks. It's working
already. I've started
to bleed. Show me, please
how to make it stop.

WIND FULL OF HOLLOWS

The air, brother, feel? It's lead
today—dawn's dull

gray haze. Gray with words
and dirt gray skin. Leaves
too, gray. This room

      *

Our boyhood fort below
the stairs, waiting footfall never

comes. I finger seconds, finger
years: Your ash, your bone,
close and cryptic as my own scruff

      *

So many rooms in a brother's
body: numbers, names, shorn

from walls.—You took blood orange
between your teeth. Tore the rind
till juice spilled your jaw

Varietal Attachment

Some spread out wide near the surface   Some sink
a taproot down deep   Some like oak seek brothers and
cousins with which to entwine   A handful hermit
on rockface and tors   A few yearn for desert   Atacama
Tanami   Other trees swill from montane lakes   Then
there are those that thrive in warm sand   In loam
Loess soil   In alluvial moraine   As well as a portion
preferring mere clay   Yet some shoots need no earth to
cling to their niche   High in tall trees with shoulders
in mist   Fingers learn to feed only on air

COLUMBARIA
after Joseph Cornell

We live in a box
built for birds. Low-ceilinged,
the kitchen once kept chickens
for beauty, peacocks
for breakfast. You may enter
without leaving your seat

*

A cupboard full of
cupboards behind blue,
blue windows—flat and endless
with contrails of flight.
What matters most has been
mislaid

*

A perch, no bird. A rod,
no drape. Not all things
can be offset or pared.
The cage unlocks
to an indigo artifice
of sky

*

A small white room—
it could be a stage—the ladder
climbs or descends
but never departs. Our parrot
is missing. The tether
remains

*

What's left of light:
A thin soiled line
divides earth from
air, the color of dirt.
What would we say if
we had something

*

to say? A storm
sweeps east. Beneath
wide eaves borne
by chained swans, I
watch the wind
chasing its tail.

WHAT I WANTED
Creeley cento

I had wanted to be of use   wanted to be lucid   my own
fool   I had wanted less   to be broken   something like sand
I had wanted to go home   that was on Thursday
there are ways beyond this place   ways to dislike you at least
as much as myself   I have always wanted to be generous
like that

Snail Phonetics

At its core is a vowel
      filled with need—a moist doughy pulp
that protracts and recoils yet

      never stops cooing, while the consonantal shell
to which words conform
      both opens and ends, gives bite to each sound

with concaved declension and
      wide thin lip. This union of difference remains
asymmetric: Short, long, rounded,

      schwa vs. plosive, affricate, bilabial,
stop. Without the one,
      no heart, no song—less the other, only goo.

Your Soft Throat

semi-cento from Sappho

I want

to give
            of light the silver

young sticky leaves

                        quick sparrows
whipping their wings

the earth   breathes
water

take your fill
                        after
            and toward

*

        emptied by birds

a deerhead lies
     ear
        to earth

I   still
    my limbs

             unwilling
    but going

        as ferns play fool

lest
        loss
    would

        would not
and I
        I

prayed   this word
want

*

and if nothing

           but going

hear again   what he did
      not say

two minds
in me   still

      our name is gone and
I

        and I

      cannot long
like this

I breathe   you
in please

      breathe
me

        out

IDYLL

Auden cento

a cloudless night like this
how still it is   dark-green

upon the distant heights
appearing unannounced

the moon   now, as desire
and the thing desired   now

through night's caressing
grip   yes, we are going

to suffer   sylvan meant
savage in those primal woods

FALLOUT

If words were runes, if numbers, iris, the pointer's ridged
whirl, if correct code, the right combination, a crocodile jaw
I could fit in my pocket—not sense, nor nonsense but under
sense, between absence and innocence, inside each pair's busy
burled pact, within plain parlance of spider, horse and dog
sense—would the knot untie, my eyes unchange, the equation
solve, could I find the phrase that slides off this rock, that
tutors a man to unstick his tail

fall in with, fall upon, fall all over

In the sentence I'm parsing, verb
piles into verb, a valence of past and

foreseen future, knees run rattletrap
as this man touches my lips, act

and actors in syntactical sequence
without punctuation, his hand

become blue light on my neck as I
mumble his jeans, losing my

language, fragments now weightless
as wind, abruptly we're glued to the

full moon's felled hare, a new
conjugation, all present tense—one

undivided I. Almost holy this spell:
To hell with Emily and her ordinary

sin, desire is abduction. When I open
my mouth, I speak only tongues

fall for

Sometimes I knew him, winsome surface of his own
invention—he was a wreck no less than I—my shame loved
his: Born into us, the collie in my nature, the spaniel, more
often hound in his

fall both, fall because, fall so so so

Burnt leaves, chimes of ice
in heavy cut glass, a brown wind

wicks away sweat—somewhere
howls, a wing-thrum of locust,
somewhere there's sleep

*

Such small lies, like termites,
no-see-ums, like minor seductions'

momentary wince—tongue
and zipper, with all those
teeth, so easily stuck

*

That other thing, the third we
were, I need to hold like a tick

in my hand—see it sidle my palm,
watch pincers attach—since
striking the match to make it let go

*

When he said—and what he
didn't—I waited for days, the leash

gone missing: I don't recall
if there was a moon, a hornet
swarm, or nothing

fall even though, fall until

All cock at dawn, a rollicking pup, a cricket's chorus of
adoration. I failed to count cuspids when he curled his bite, or
confess to myself I'd been declared coney, that I chewed my
own tail. Later I learned the limits of language—and rabbits
aren't really for friendship but food

fall short, fall back, fall behind

I beg, I bark, stick spikes in his feet,
bind his hair to a bed
with barbed wire, I pace smudged

fingers up bare screaming thighs.
Maybe it's the American
in me, maybe the child, this little loss

I refuse to see small. I'd bolt if I
could, would jackal
my lack, but there's less of me left

than meets the eye, a dog's hind leg
unable to shake its
rabbity dream. I've merely locked him

away so he'll never walk, so we'll talk
every day and always
trade colds, so I'll never need proof

62

of devotion. Still the worm proceeds
with want's damp pant
as I shred the emails that soil my cage.

Like Medea's black cloak, what we
said and we did blister
my skin—beautiful as it burns

fall away, fall apart

His face in light streaming through glass, white glow of
morning without vestige or depth—I almost believe in his
snug secret life: I am watching him sleep, his face in repose,
I am watching him breathe—half-here, half-blank, beguiling
and broken

falling, falling, freefall

SUMMER'S END

Jarrell cento

summer   sunset   someone is playing
some of the sky is gray   some of it is white

the torn hillside with its crooked hands
a cow wandering the bare field

a fox lifts his head from feathers
there are fens beyond   the world there obeys

stretched out under oak   in the wood's new leaves
the sky darkened watching you

when I looked at the tree the bough was still shaking
it is evening   one bat whirls

a shadow is floating through moonlight
not to have guessed is better   what is, ends

Changing Your Mind

Nothing suggests you will. The disadvantage
of knowing you so long is knowing you

don't make decisions without due thought.
You want to be nice: It's not hard work
being the man you already are—but who cares

for good form when feeling this limp.
Let's have some blame, some lamps

with wings. Let's have in the neighbors
and put on a show—you wear Hush Puppies,
I'll wear cleats. I admit you're good:

If I'd given what you really required—devoted
indifference—we wouldn't be here (or

anywhere together). Lost socks, left
shoes: I always hoped we'd hold tight to each
other—a counterpoise of one-legged men—

shambling forward as if we were whole.
Only you don't read love poems and mine

set forks where they should serve spoons.
Should I find a strop? Or lose the mask?
Ought I have more pride or say it out loud:

I'd rather be here, even now, than to have
been always nowhere without you.

LISTENING TO WORDSWORTH

semi-cento from Philip Larkin & William Wordsworth

Before he woke to an earth-sweet scent—

      the rainwash rush from a brook below,

    before the thought,   Storm's stopped.
                          The sky, white clay.

     Before Larkin, rain-blind, drove
                into the ditch:

There was a time
                on a road
                  near Hull, the poet speeding
    in early spring rain

                 things which I have seen I
       can see no more

        wipes the windscreen, thick with mist,
              loudens the BBC's voice

    when the heavens are bare

rising and
      falling through tonsured
           hills, through narrow hedgerows

      from the fields of sleep

his joy on first hearing
        that poem, the cane   when he forgot

       sullen

while Earth herself is adoring

as wipers swish,
his breath, the fog

shades of the prison-house begin to close
the growing Boy

pushed aside by his own life
into velvet

folds, over well-worn heights

forget the glories he hath known

repeating paths of races of sheep

sequestered
safely in crofts, safely now
in abandoned byres—

holds himself against emotion, against
the flood of
first affections

clouding, he squints for the road

the sallies of his mother's kisses

with the butt of his palm
tries to rub the glass clear, to
clear his eyes

some fragment *of human life*

then weeps outright

as if his whole vocation

                                   were endless   imitation

                  that shows

                          nothing

sing, ye Birds, sing, sing a joyous song!

                                   and is nowhere

                    let the young Lambs bound

                                   and is endless

                  nothing can bring back the hour

          the thought of high windows,
deep blue air,

                  what remains—

SEA OF LOVE

Emily D. and Odysseus are nobody too,
        though Jesse says they're daft, says we,
you and I both, says everyone here is
        Somebody. Say it!—*I am...*

Now duck. Being somebody would sure
        be nice, having front-facing sight and
teeth that tear. But a nobody's dewy,
        ungulate eyes hazard far less. Even Zeus

hid from Hera in the form of a bull.
        Trust a somebody to say that living
in limbo is not real life, to ask if
        you'll poke out your head in the path

of a scythe. Luckily nobodies know
        they don't need to fall when they're
already flat—there's nothing wrong
        with a sole's-eye view. Only love

and water go that low, always
        descending—all rivers, all lakes
are nobodies too, losing their names
        as they enter the sea.

MAKING SENSE

Only thirty years more used-up
than me—except her mouth
makes a newborn's "O."

Mother fingers my hand as if
dandling a doll. Wants to—
cannot—wants to, remember.

Traces a thumb. Nuzzles
the palm, breathing its scent.
Cradles my hand close

to her chin. Cannot—wants
to—almost, remembers: tiny nails
so perfect they already scratch.

DOULA

I am too old for this—too old
        to lose myself in a cloud-forest jungle
made up for the screen, to mug,

grunt, to pound my chest, go
        ōō-ōō like the fake great apes
in this very bad movie. But here

am I, suddenly departing my body,
        doffing sheer skin for their dark
plush shag. Call it turncoat, hightail,

call it regress, even grift—or merely
        madness. These made-up gorillas
keep pulling me in, displacing the chill

of my solitary room. They reach
        with rough hands, strong arms—give
air, release, they offer their brand

of prehensile love, a nest on their family's
        broad-shouldered branch—calling,
whooping, *ōō-ōō-ōō* as they tug me

through. They have what I've missed,
        what I wish—no, knew—must exist.
They've come for me finally—*ōō*—

they're bringing me home. Where
        I'll never know shame, never
feel my self many, never fear

to grow old. Where we'll always be
        together. Where I'll never be alone—
ōō-ōō-ōōōō-ōō

Harvest

Some only boys, but all resembled old men peeing at
a village latrine, their buttocks trembling like the sad
lips of camels at sup—that's when they shot them.
Then lime white as sugar. The bodies planted too
shallow, it seemed, for trees or corn to sprout.

*

When wolves take a caribou down they are casual
butchers: Ripping a shoulder still running, they harry
the hocks, strafe heaving ribs from a close, sedulous
trot, then circle the beast like children playing musical
chairs.

*

Mother recalls it rained that spring for the first time
in years. Summer followed, rank and hot, the ground
swollen, giddy with green. At harvest, months later—
limbs, ears—no one went hungry.

*

Sometimes dismembered, the calf bleats a long
time, its mother a witness nearby. No different than
gunmen, really, though wolves bear no malice, while
men leave the meat behind.

WHAT YOU NAME

To bear a name is to claim an exact mode of collapse
- E. M. Cioran

Banana trees little more than my height,
abundant with clusters of green fingers
nestled among dark scrotal pods, are
what I noticed for weeks. Then I saw
a "seedpod" move. *Bats*, I was told.

*

In the Hebrew Bible words
begin creation—rouse the world
into sound, into sense (thereby sin).

*

Maybe not denial, but something
missing (a hole unplumbed, unfilled)
when a family suffers for lack of a name.
Then someone says, *Alcoholic*—thereafter
the word's tattooed on their tongues.

*

How could I tell a carrot from
a cat if I had no words? Know
what to grate, which to pet?

*

The Ilongot people of the Philippines
name orchids after the human body—
their world is lush and never lonely.
They say: *There blooms a thigh, a breast,*
here toenails, an ear, yonder elbows and thumbs.

*

I hold up a toothbrush for my aphasic mother
to ask her its name. *Soap*, she says
slowly. I hold up a soapbar: *Corned beef.*

*

Once I said to myself, *Worry*, when
you stopped patting my shoulder, when you
rolled away in your sleep. By and by I thought,
Middle-age, or *Needs space.* Now, because
you told me (for once I was listening),
I know our new name: *Over.*

*

At last Marco Polo beheld
a rhinoceros in the cage of a Khan.
He called it, *Unicorn.* Later, *Beast.*

Undertow

Poor passion, you bear the blame
and perhaps it's deserved. But not
this time: The perp's a Caspar. Blame

Midwest moderation, blame caution,
blame niceness, patience, blame
wisdom and sloth both, blame fear.

No cannonball crash from a highdive—
we dipped our toes in the kiddie's,
wading for years with nary a splash

before changing to swim. So brazenly
tepid! So prudently rash! I thought
I'd unman the family connubial curse,

bargain for forever to paddle the tide.
So blame forgetting that even in
shallows it's possible to drown.

ANATOMY OF COUPLING

semi-cento from Armand Marie Leroi,
Sir Thomas Browne & Leonardo da Vinci

1.

ostrich eggs porcelain a baby's tight fist

the rule of matter begins with a will to combine

7 days after conception a human embryo begins to dig

mutation and beauty begin as chance

2.

the devices of desire their imperfect objects
their marvelous volition

a world about which I know so little
the womb's the obscure walls the origin of deformity
of attraction the purpose of loss the instructions
needed to make a man

each human embryo holds more than a 100 mutations

if we had no need if none felt alone if all
unbroken not error nor fall but simply the price

3.

the first cut the second the infinite
forms contained therein

as to the calculus of coupling the constant measure
of devotion must not be subtracted
and never be shared

in a mathematically perfect universe
you and I would have never been born

about mutation of affections we cannot deny it
in hares and men

4.

the lost language of two like a tribe gone extinct a life
the longing our stories our songs

for 18 days nothing a white oval disc one millimeter long
only 10 days more a head a gut a spine lungs
inside no less harmonic than snails

nature disrupts its own perfection

to love or be loved always unworthy and never
returned if I had to choose

5.

easy to mistake a bone for a rock to forget
bone once was alive as a heart

there is beauty in monstrosity

on day 21 cycloptic and mute it begins to beat

how the need to marvel, to marvel
with, endures

When We Dig

Trees had long borne fruit by then—hung green and untroubled, rinds still hard, still not quite sweet—eighty thousand years ago among the Zagros Mountains when the hole was first dug in the Shanidar Cave. Inside the earth was damp from yesterday's rain as men of his clan scraped away crust to open soft soil below, alive with grubs and worms, telling stories as they dug.

While village women in the valley below, reverently chanting, washed the cold, bruised flesh with aurok fat. His skin and plaited hair grew supple, making old wounds, long-healed, shine like jagged letters inscribed in hide (though of course these hominids had no writing). Soon after, they bound his legs and arms in a tight fetal clasp with gut so he might return to earth's womb in the manner he came.

Yet before he was buried facing west, before dried meat and herbs, before the mallet, flint, and other talismans he would need were placed inside the hole, his kin strewed flowers— what we call yarrow, cornflower and ragwort, woody horsetail, hollyhock and St. Barnaby's thistle—to decorate his tomb and begin their tribe's death charm. It may be that those gathered, with their thick bodies and brows, their high thin voices, touched each other's backs or hands as they filled in the pit. A few may even have wept.

*

Kept cool by strangers for nearly two weeks, my brother's body could not be buried until his estranged third wife signed the release. Only then could we gather in the far northeast corner of the cemetery in Anniston, Alabama, where my family's plot commands the rise, his last wife's ample bust served-up in hot pink spandex above tight black capris, clutching his dog (who would not stop barking) as his three-year-old daughter, giddy and humming, danced on the white marble markers before the backhoe went to work.

*

As for the hole: Some paleontologists now say a Neanderthal could not see a self when he looked in a river, never knew guilt, self-doubt, could not feel grief, was never free to betray his kin, his gods or even himself. A few of his kind may even have eaten each other. Thus death came to these bipeds and went, noticed no more than would our cattle at graze. Seen in this light, the ditch was ill-dug, the bones haphazard, the flowers a later human corruption, or more likely were brought by Persian jirds (small rodents, still extant, known to store seeds when they burrow).

KNOT

The monogamy of crows and
cardinals tells me nothing

*

Morning blown brittle, unable
to gather, unable to hold heat

*

Most mammals live solitary
lives except when they breed

*

A successful imitation of
marriage is marriage, or is it

*

No one thing is one thing only,
then come bonobos and men

*

If you want me
to love you—leave

Putting Down the Dog

This lust for explanation,
for reasons that sate. As if

disorder weren't ordinary fare,
enigma colostrum, quandary
dessert. As if a woman

puts down her prized Peke
which bit her so the cause

could come clear, before asking
herself for the 100th time today why
her gay husband left. Soon

sliced apart, tissue and lymph
dissected, blood tested, cells

cultured, the root is revealed:
Rabies. Tumor. Bad breeding.
Lax training. Maybe just

an off day. How good to find
a fine hard edge, undogged

by unknowns—as if a mind
would relax once fed. Not-
withstanding the dog dead and

in pieces. His bed still empty.
The collar useless as answers.

FUGUE
semi-cento from Donald Justice

1.
His face more than others—
thirty years and more.

Not vague smoke, legato
strings. Certain moments

never change, never stop
being, like birthmarks

and burns. That afternoon,
snow, and no flowers.

Telephone poles where
there should have been trees.

2.
He sat with hands folded,
speaking of islands, barren

beach. Dune after dune.
Sunshine just then, wind

and more snow. Long
fingers in cold yellow

light. Trees without
leaves. It was possible

then. Now comes evening—
an odd noisy silence.

3.
Look, he said. A baby
boy with an old

man's face. The light
gone yellow. More

snow, no flowers.
A woodwind echoes

beyond the trees. Did
one of us cry?—Again

the oboe's Möbius
moan. Like memory.

4.
A broken tooth. How
sunlight caught his hair.

Yellow, unwilling to let
go. So little is needed. We

made the bed. Our sheets
chalk white. It was still

possible. No others.
Wind and afternoon

snow. No leaves. No face
to forget. No noise.

FOREST, NO TREES

I didn't see it—
there, behind dark firs.
I didn't not see it
either. Felt it, rather.
Almost white. Almost
light, but not just light.
Thick like water
though not really water.
It couldn't have been
water. More like fire
held aloft for a moment,
its shudder and glint.
Or sound. Suspended
above, quivering
like an echo. Yet
piercing, too. So loud
if there had been
sound it would almost
have hurt. You
trembled. You held me.
Your scarf was ice-blue.
We were there—
remember?—Then
we weren't.

The Innocence of Apples

This Chicago morning, humdrum like most others,
awkward to ignite as a limp, damp match. As I bend
for the *Trib* neighbors wave by rote. My dog fails

to wag as I open the fridge. No one at my house
cares where I slept last night. Even the perfect
Red Delicious I munch is bland as cellophane.

Rooting through the bin you left I find a jumble
of heirlooms—Haralson, Hawkeye, Northern
Spy, though I snatch the homely Black Twig.

This apple has heft, furls a dark stem like a flag
on the 4th yet chastely curls to cup the soft
tuft below. When I bite into its ordinary skin—

a pause, resistant, almost a pulse before the
prick—juice floods my tongue, a tart, pulpy
sweet, redolent of sin.

EARTHSONG
  for Kathleen Ferrier

Perhaps that day, impossibly blue,
Sarasota Bay glimmered bottomless

and good, turquoise glass unbroken
by current and wind. Perhaps as she drove

home that day with her radio on,
past palms, jacaranda, amaranth and

sea grape, Julia, my aunt, heard a voice call
like warm autumn rain, like the indigo

echo of night at dawn, like her mother's
cupped hands—calling and calling—above

the engine's low thrum. Perhaps the music
still hadn't ceased as she eased the car

inside her garage then lowered the door
—listening—let the motor lull: Found,

perhaps, the shadows there soothing,
found Mahler's dark-soiled song

enfolding her close, found air, her
tongue, tasting of loam, tasting of silt—

sound filling her body with nightblue
drift, filling her lungs with alluvial

root—calling, calling—her heart
beyond surfeit, so full of deep

bloom—calling her—so suddenly
full of earth's rapt green hum.

How the Planets Maintain Orbit

Sixteen hours is all it took
for a freshman *dom* in a dorm
twelve blocks away to find his *sub*

and begin the cutting. Nothing savage—
just slender lines carved in bark

of a girl's tender skin to speak of love
everlasting. Like moose in rut, monarchs
bound for Mexico, like old men at

my mother's nursing home when staff
unwitting, turn away and she welcomes

them in. *Was your mother always like this?*
the nun without habit asks. I think, *Before
she lost half her brain?*—but mutter lamely,

She's lonely. I'm ashamed of myself,
ashamed I lied. *Yes, Sister,* I should have

said, *Like every body ever born. Like you
inside your soft pale skin. Like me, yes.
Always like this, thank God. Yes.*

QUESTION OF EGGS

The old joke Woody Allen stole for the end of *Annie
Hall*—about the guy who goes to a shrink regarding
his brother who thinks he's a chicken—that's really
about things we need like sex and love which are no
less cracked.

Hart Crane writes, *Paradise is not a question of eggs.*
Though wouldn't Eden be one sure place with a cache
of eggs? Or did Hart mean one's brother's eggs always
make sense in Shangri-La? Even that heaven requires
no eggs to be perfect?

If our eggs *were* sensible and easy to control, could they
still grant moments of idiot transport and goofball
oneness? Of spangle-eyed spastic release? Still give
comfort, purpose, that dopey grateful aching peace?

Meanwhile I'm heartsore and hungry. I'll hold off the
latter with a Denver omelet, except solitude's solution
is not so easy. *In your dreams you can have your eggs cooked
as perfectly as you want*, says Anna Freud, *but you cannot
eat them.*

I hope that's not true. I smell bacon frying, and from
my brother's room, hear: *Bok-bok-bok-bWAAK!*

WAIT
for Retha Schlabach

They don't care for us
        or wear coathanger haloes,

    they don't bear wings and dirt
           clings to their feet.

      Flight alone

         never made a thing
   holy. Yet sometimes

somehow
      in the chimney-flue space

    between soil and sky
  air breaks
              open—

easy, unburdened
         the moon escapes
     a pail of black water,

   a wing-rush of bees
      eclipses the sun,

         and antelope leap
    leaving the ground
      on wind-borne limbs—

as if weight suspended
        the earthbound rise:

   Maybe like clouds

                              they cover us
                    all, maybe

              like rain
they return.

COME ALONG NOW

semi-cento from Sylvia Plath for her son Nick, 1962-2009

Your savage baby mouth, Nicholas,
how you ate me alive—the one
solid thing, your junkie devotion.

No, dear one, you couldn't save me—
that's the boy in you speaking.
Much too hungry, I gorged

on myself. For you I prayed
the wit to let go. In your white
highchair, I let you go early—you

barely one—I hoped you'd learn
to let me go too. My baby
in the barn, I don't blame you—

your sacramental rage too much
like my own, the soft-headed guilt's
pure Ted. You'll see him soon

though you really won't
care. Letting go is ugly labor.
I think of you searching out larch

in a forest of pine. And the fish,
your fish—it's them you'll miss most,
fat snail, your death-mad salmon.

How you loved their rose-bodied
spawn, their end/beginning
a Siamese twin. Likewise your friends,

your guardian sister, adoring—all
weeping, convicting themselves and
me—don't know how to let go.

Bald white days, the mirrors sheeted.
No need fear my twice-wrecked womb.
The pain you woke to isn't yours

anymore. Come along now Nick,
my candlestick son: Over your body
the clouds go—all cool, all blue.

OBEDIENCE SCHOOL

Unlike my father, this stumpy-
legged dog with over-sized ears
never gives up hope. My dad
sometimes kicked our old mongrel,

twenty years later I once did too—
different dog, same rage.
Five minutes later the setter
simpered back to lick my foot.

Tonight my dog and I obey
our drill: Pat his head, switch
the light, retire to our beds.
Still his tail thump-thumps

for another treat. It's ludicrous
his hope, though it's my aspiration
too—learning to sit, stay, to offer
my belly unguarded, lick the soft

pink lipstick below my tail without
shame or compulsion, to wag
as if I believe the world waits
eager with one more bone.

OVERCOME BY THE BEAUTY OF LOSS
I WRITE A POEM ABOUT THE DEATH OF LI PO
CALLED "NIGHTBOAT ON THE YANGTZE"

Drunk again. You
sing to ink-dark

water and dance
for the moon.

Leaning, you slip
your hand inside

her lotus-white
robe. The river

opens. Flowing
together, you

drift ten-thousand
nights to the

blue jade sea.

SONNET II
Berrigan cento

On the green   a white boy goes
he's braver than I, brother   the trees
breathless blue   stand stark-naked
a fat black woman   singing a song
I fell on my knees   because closed air
because the blue day   a man full of
clocks   full of necessary lies   dull black
breakage   where ripeness begins   is there room
in this room   I don't know   where anything
I don't know   where the door will open
which side of the blue   how strange to be
done   I am closing my window   because
mud white   because everything   a brown
desk   a blue shirt   because

PRETTY, PRETTY

three ladies say
looking down

at my mother,
Isn't she pretty!

though not as a question—
her sister, cousin,

long-time friend June
with raven-dyed do—

She was always so pretty,
in the white angora

sweater I chose
pink lipstick and blush,

her platinum hair,
Oh Pretty, oh pretty

like chickadee chirps,
the trio so close

their pastels mesh,
while Mom's famous

pooched lips and
off-center smile

now stretch
symmetric

to store-brand
stupor she'd dub

in a facelift,
Bad work. Still

the ladies watch
over, lean in-

to each other,
widows, all three

passing these words
like food to

their chicks, like
teens their

tongues, like breath
for the drowned,

So pretty, so pretty
their shape-

note song,
Pretty, pretty

Pretty, pretty
their prayer.

EXULTATE

O toe-tickler, sun-licker
O green-tongued graze-giver, wind-waver,
       swale-swadler, wide-swathed worldweed
O fodder-father, field-feeder, dung-drop, dew-dryer,
       deep down drizzle-drunk
O broad bed of repose for lamb and fawn

Hear me dream pillow, you verdant divan
Hear me, O viridescent duvet
Let me lie upon your broad bosky belly
Let me breathe your musk still drowsy and damp, still moist
       as my sheets
Let me feel your root and warmth once more, the curve
       of your shaft as you rise at first light
O, let me bring my lips to each blade
       and bray for more

FEAST

Below—fat sighs, the far
glazed earth, a clatter and wheeze of

concrete skin, of trade, of truck, the
hammer and snare, small scuttle and dart

of dull animal ache, a buzzard bloat of easy
oxygen where everything is everything else

and I forget slicing each breath with my
tongue's deft tip. While above—dry

teeth, sulphur, faint scent
of peat and rock spines

arched against fading
vault-blue, split at

20,000 feet where
rope and axe

bite slow: Here
hypoxic breathing

comes fast and
flat, gasping

hics of scanty
air, loud

blood-beat
and isolate

sight, where
not appetite

but sense
swells

and un-
snarls—the

tooth
and tang

of wind—
clouds—

cold—of
white—

of light—
the lull—

blue
lips—a

hush—
the still—

a taste
at

last
of

full—

No-Good, Low-Life, Low-Down Love

Not a white porcelain cup
in the middle of a table,
sturdy and safe—but
a tall crystal tumbler, full-to-tipping, perched at the table's far
edge, how the glass glows
with late afternoon light while a crack
traced in silver
cuts down the near side, how
my eyes don't blink as the gash seems to
grow, how this moment
extends while the filigree spreads, fine veins
branching beyond and
beyond as a small bead of water, bulging to brim, shimmers
its descent. How, suddenly
I can't move. How, soon it will
shatter. How I feel so
alive.

What Sappho Knew

Even if Sappho
glided serenely

through Edo's
floating world

her white
silk kimono

spilling
chrysanthemum

petals hushed
in her wake, if

her want coursed
to men, her

ink to koans
rather than

verse, if Sappho
died by blade

instead of
a leap—beyond

oceans and
epochs, despite

differing tongues,
still she would

know the clear
sound of water,

graceful and
lithe, how it

flows like
desire wherever

it will, maunders
through fields

pierced by
new rice, slips

beneath
walls and

seeps into
rock, where

silent while
kneeling

on moss-
felted stones,

Sappho would
cup cool

water to her
lips as if

kissing
a child or

soothing a
fever, just as

with each
infant grown

too soon and
each thing

fiercely loved,
how she would

open
her fingers

to let water
go

WHAT COMES AFTER

A kingfisher flares up from the trees,
lodgepole and fir—soon disappears.
Sweat feels cool against my backpack
clanking with cans of peaches and beer

*

I'm beginning to think that I'm glad
I left, glad I've come

*

Across the gray glass lake emerging
from mist, a pair of Clark's grebes
glides into view. If there's effort
in their movement, it's nothing I see

*

Side by side they drift closer, twins
from this distance

*

What came before I cannot know, nor
what comes after—whether the marsh
goes salt, the grebe's eggs grow frail,
the nearby owl dines on their young

*

Nor can I tell if the dance they've
begun is a test the male will fail

*

As morning grows clear, their courtship
gains pace, each motion a mirror, each sound
repercussed. Maybe later they'll mate
though this too I won't see. Yet today

*

for a moment, I believe in movement,
I believe in poise, in the twining

*

of necks, the flaring of wings, in a perfect
paired quickstep across the blue face
of water, in holding my breath while
the far-fetched comes true.

TEACHING A MAN TO UNSTICK HIS TAIL

NOTES & ACKNOWLEDGMENTS

Deep gratitude to all the poets, teachers, friends, and readers who have contributed to this books' gestation, birth, early and ongoing education—critiquing, correcting, encouraging, suggesting, inspiring—including but certainly not limited to: Jane Fulton Alt, Priscilla Atkins, Virginia Bell, Charles & Marjorie Benton, April Bernard, Jan Bottiglieri, Ann Brandon, Terry Breitwiser, Coleman & Irene Brown, David Buddha-Hargarten, Ken Carls, Sarah Carson, Grady Chambers, Helen Degen Cohen, Nina Corwin, Bill Coughlin, David Csicsko, Carol Eding, Bob Faust, Paul Florian, Alice George, Amy Gerstler, Gail Goepfert, Scott Gordon, Louise Grant, Chris Green, Joseph Anglin Hamilton, Charlotte Hart, Peter Hawkins, Mary Hawley, Jane Henderson, Christine Herzer, Deborah Holloway, Larry Janowski, Catharine Jones, David Jones, Ami Kaye, Bonnie Kepplinger, Bill Lampkin, Jay Lattin, Timothy Liu, Mike McNulty, Susan Merrell, Vern Miller, Ed Ochester, Elise Packard, Gary Pavela, Jeffrey Perkins, Bill Pinsoff, Mike Puican, Jamie Quatro, Miodrag Radulovacki, Liam Rector, Spencer Reece, Harold Richman, Deborah Nodler Rosen, Jacob Saenz, David Scronce, Tracey Shafroth, Peter & Ronnie Siegel, Barry Silesky, Andrea Witzke Slot, Doug Stapleton, Joyce Sutphen, Susan Page Tillett, Angela Narciso Torres, Tony Trigilio, David Trinidad, Michael Tsalka, Valerie Wallace, Chris Walker, Sarah Wetzel, Jackie White, Ian Williams, Joan Wynn, and Mary K. Young. Many thanks to the Art Institute of Chicago for permitting the use of the Lucian Freud painting. And my special thanks to Bryan Borland and the team at SRP!

"Wait" and "With(out) Him" appeared previously in *Pyrene's Fountain*. "The Mother, Broken" appeared previously in *Cutbank*.

About the Author

Ralph Hamilton is editor of *RHINO*. He has an MFA in Poetry from Bennington. His poems have appeared in *Court Green*, *CutBank*, *Pirene's Fountain*, *Blackbird*, and other journals. He has had residencies at Ragdale and the Anderson Center, and later served on the board of the Ragdale Foundation. He was judge for *Fifth Wednesday Journal*'s prize in poetry in Fall 2013, and guest poetry editor for *Fifth Wednesday*'s Fall 2014 issue. Ralph lives in Evanston, Illinois, with his son.

About the Press

Sibling Rivalry Press is an independent publishing house based in Little Rock, Arkansas. Our mission is to publish work that disturbs and enraptures.

www.siblingrivalrypress.com

Gratitude

This book was produced, in part, due to the support of the non-profit Sibling Rivalry Press Foundation. The Sibling Rivalry Press Foundation supports small presses and small press authors through grants and fiscal sponsorship.

www.srpfoundation.org

CPSIA information can be obtained at www.ICGtesting.com
Printed in the USA
LVOW02s2030260215

428380LV00007B/66/P